IT'S TIME TO EAT CELERY

It's Time to Eat Celery

Walter the Educator

Silent King Books
A WhichHead Entertainment Imprint

Copyright © 2024 by Walter the Educator

All rights reserved. No part of this book may be reproduced in any manner whatsoever without written per- mission except in the case of brief quotations embodied in critical articles and reviews.

First Printing, 2024

Disclaimer

This book is a literary work; the story is not about specific persons, locations, situations, and/or circumstances unless mentioned in a historical context. Any resemblance to real persons, locations, situations, and/or circumstances is coincidental. This book is for entertainment and informational purposes only. The author and publisher offer this information without warranties expressed or implied. No matter the grounds, neither the author nor the publisher will be accountable for any losses, injuries, or other damages caused by the reader's use of this book. The use of this book acknowledges an understanding and acceptance of this disclaimer.

It's Time to Eat a Celery is collectible early learning book by Walter the Educator suitable for all ages belonging to Walter the Educator's Time to Eat Book Series. Collect more books at WaltertheEducator.com

USE THE EXTRA SPACE TO TAKE NOTES AND DOCUMENT YOUR MEMORIES

CELERY

The sun is shining, warm and bright,

It's Time to Eat
Celery

It's lunchtime now, what a happy sight!

I see a plate, what could it be?

A crunchy green snack just waiting for me!

It's long and tall, a lovely stick,

Let's take a bite, oh, not too quick!

It's celery, crisp and cool and green,

The best veggie snack I've ever seen.

Crunch, crunch, munch away,

Celery makes for a fun-filled day!

Each bite a snap, so crisp and loud,

It's the kind of crunch that makes you proud.

Let's dip it in peanut butter, smooth,

Or with some hummus, oh, how it soothes!

Maybe just plain, it's yummy too,

A veggie treat, perfect for you.

It's Time to Eat

Celery

I love how fresh it tastes, so light,

It makes me feel so strong and bright!

Celery sticks are such a treat,

It's always fun when it's time to eat.

It grows in gardens, tall and straight,

With leaves so green, isn't it great?

Farmers pick it when it's tall,

So we can enjoy it, one and all.

Celery's good for you, did you know?

It helps you grow, from head to toe!

It's packed with water, fresh and cool,

It's Time to Eat

Celery

And gives you strength, so you can rule!

When you eat your celery stick,

You'll feel so smart, and healthy quick!

It's a veggie that's full of fun,

A crunchy snack for everyone!

So next time it's time for a bite,

Pick up some celery, take delight!

With every munch, you'll feel so good,

It's Time to Eat

Celery

Like a healthy superhero should!

Crunch, crunch, one more piece,

Celery's joy will never cease!

Let's share it with friends, a snack to share,

Eating celery shows we care!

ABOUT THE CREATOR

Walter the Educator is one of the pseudonyms for Walter Anderson. Formally educated in Chemistry, Business, and Education, he is an educator, an author, a diverse entrepreneur, and he is the son of a disabled war veteran. "Walter the Educator" shares his time between educating and creating. He holds interests and owns several creative projects that entertain, enlighten, enhance, and educate, hoping to inspire and motivate you. Follow, find new works, and stay up to date with Walter the Educator™

at WaltertheEducator.com

Milton Keynes UK
Ingram Content Group UK Ltd.
UKHW051141031124
450424UK00019B/1095